P9-BYH-868

Garfield gains weight

BY: JIM DAVIS

BALLANTINE BOOKS · NEW YORK

COPYRIGHT © 1981 BY UNITED FEATURES SYNDICATE, INC.

ALL RIGHTS RESERVED UNDER INTERNATIONAL AND PAN-AMERICAN COPYRIGHT CONVENTIONS. PUBLISHED IN THE UNITED STATES BY BALLANTINE BOOKS, A DIVISION OF RANDOM HOUSE, INC., NEW YORK, AND SIMULTANEOUSLY IN CANADA BY RANDOM HOUSE OF CANADA, LIMITED, TORONTO, CANADA.

LIBRARY OF CONGRESS CATALOG CARD NUMBER: 80-69730

ISBN 0-345-28844-0

MANUFACTURED IN THE UNITED STATES OF AMERICA

FIRST BALLANTINE BOOKS EDITION MARCH 1981

3 4 5 6 7 8 9

"This is the funniest book I've ever read...."

—JIM DAVIS

"This is the funniest book he's ever read...."

—CAROLYN DAVIS, Jim's Wife

"Spectacular...blockbuster ...a sure bestseller."

—JULIE HAMILTON, Jim's Business Manager

"...really average."

—VALETTE HILDEBRAND, Jim's Assistant

"It's such a nice book. He's such a nice boy."

—BETTY DAVIS, Jim's Mother

"This is the best book I ever read. This is the only book I ever read."

—DAVE "DOC" DAVIS, Jim's Brother

"This should do 'til he finds work."

—JAMES W. DAVIS, Jim's Father

"...goo, goo...ha, ha, ha."

—ALEX DAVIS, Jim's Son

JIM DAVIS
© 1981 United Feature Syndicate, Inc.

TELEVISION CAN BE HABIT FORMING
JIM DAVIS
© 1979 United Feature Syndicate, Inc.

I'VE BEEN WATCHING IT ALL DAY
1-23

WOULD YOU LIKE ME TO TURN THE TV ON, GARFIELD?
THAT WOULD BE NICE

© 1979 United Feature Syndicate, Inc.

I HATE TELEVISION
© 1979 United Feature Syndicate, Inc.
1-26
THERE ARE TOO MANY COMMERCIALS, RERUNS AND GAME SHOWS
JIM DAVIS
THE EIGHT HOURS I WATCHED YESTERDAY WAS TERRIBLE
TELEVISION IS ONLY SO MUCH MINDLESS DRIVEL...
© 1979 United Feature Syndicate, Inc.
1-27
GLOSSY ADVENTURES, SEX AND VIOLENCE
AIN'T IT GREAT?
JIM DAVIS

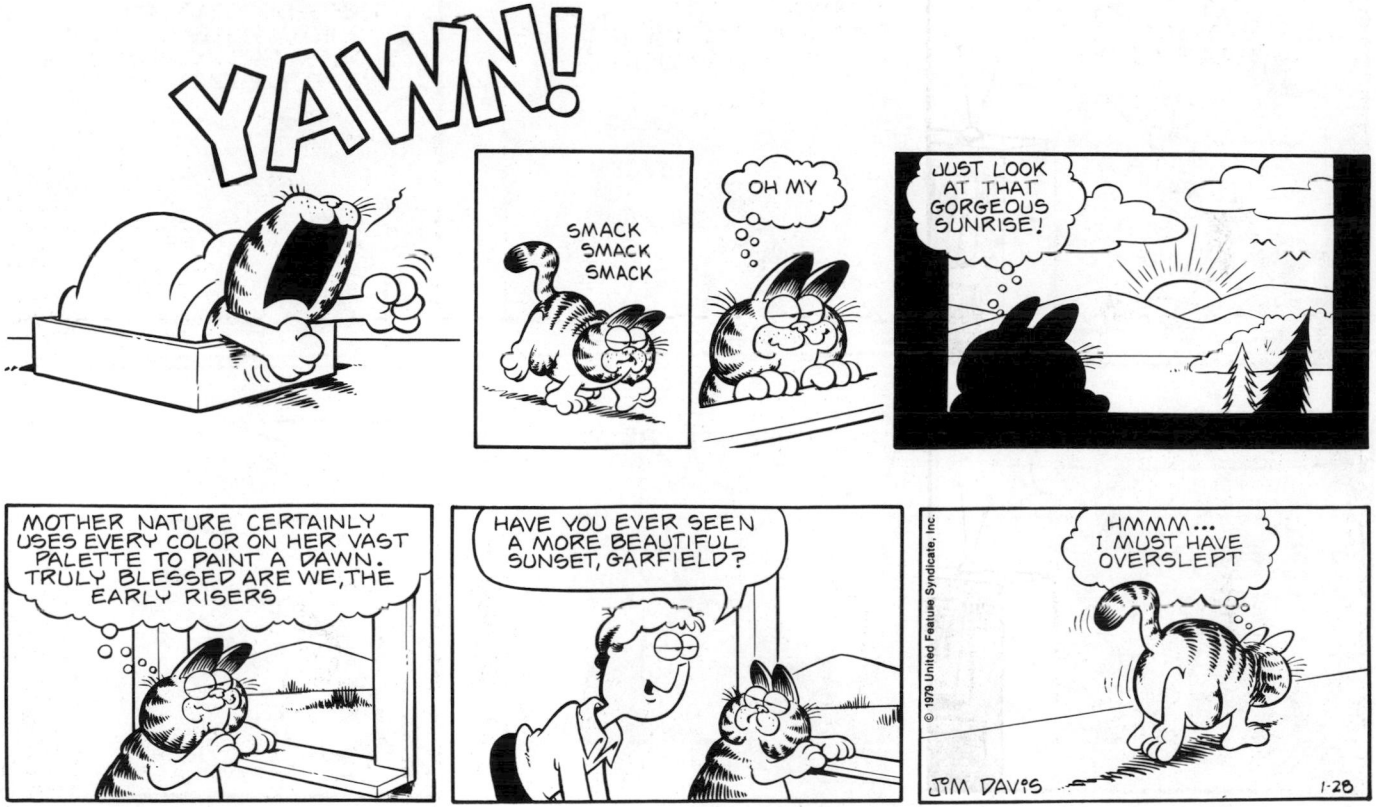
YAWN!
SMACK SMACK SMACK
OH MY
JUST LOOK AT THAT GORGEOUS SUNRISE!
MOTHER NATURE CERTAINLY USES EVERY COLOR ON HER VAST PALETTE TO PAINT A DAWN. TRULY BLESSED ARE WE, THE EARLY RISERS
HAVE YOU EVER SEEN A MORE BEAUTIFUL SUNSET, GARFIELD?
HMMM... I MUST HAVE OVERSLEPT
© 1979 United Feature Syndicate, Inc.
JIM DAVIS
1-28

GARFIELD, YOU ARE DISGUSTINGLY, SLOVENLY, SLOPPY FAT
1-29

POOR JON

HE OBVIOUSLY HAS DISGUSTINGLY, SLOVENLY, SLOPPY FAT CONFUSED WITH "BIG-BONED"
JIM DAVIS
© 1979 United Feature Syndicate, Inc.

BRENDA, MEET GARFIELD
HI, GARFIELD
© 1979 United Feature Syndicate, Inc.

IS GARFIELD A PIG?
HE'S A CAT
1-30

OH, THAT REALLY HURTS
JIM DAVIS

1-31
AHHH

CRASH!

FACE IT, GARFIELD. WINDOWSILLS JUST AREN'T BUILT FOR US QUEEN-SIZED FELINES
© 1979 United Feature Syndicate, Inc.
JIM DAVIS

IF YOU TAKE ONE BITE OF MY PIE, GARFIELD, I'LL SMACK YOUR FAT LITTLE PAWS
2-1
© 1979 United Feature Syndicate, Inc.

IF I CAN'T HAVE IT, NEITHER CAN HE
JIM DAVIS

I'LL BET YOU CAN'T WAIT TO SEE WHAT KIND OF CAT FOOD YOU'RE HAVING FOR DINNER
I'LL BET I CAN
© 1979 United Feature Syndicate, Inc.

HERE IT COMES...
YOU CAN CUT THE TENSION WITH A KNIFE
LIVER
2-2

LIVER!
OH, HOORAY, HOP ABOUT, CLAP PAWS, SQUEAL WITH GLEE
LIVER
JIM DAVIS

NOW I WOULDN'T SAY YOU'RE FAT, GARFIELD...
2-3

BUT WHEN YOU SIT AROUND THE SOFA, YOU SIT AROUND THE SOFA

HEADS, HE LIVES. TAILS, HE DIES
KICK!
JIM DAVIS
© 1979 United Feature Syndicate, Inc.

© 1979 United Feature Syndicate, Inc.
2-4

LET'S SEE... IODINE, BAND-AIDS, GAUZE, BULLWHIP, SMALL STRAIT-JACKET, HELMET, PAN, SHAMPOO, GLOVES, RINSE, CONDITIONER, BLOW DRYER, BRASS KNUCKLES, TOWEL, ROPE, ELBOW PADS...
JIM DAVIS

GARFIELD'S BATH DAY?
GARFIELD'S BATH DAY

I THINK I'LL DO SOME JOGGING
© 1979 United Feature Syndicate, Inc.
2-5

OKAY... GO, FEET!

HMMM, RECKON THE LITTLE SUCKERS JUST WEREN'T IN THE MOOD
JIM DAVIS

GARFIELD, I'D APPRECIATE IT IF YOU WOULDN'T READ OVER MY SHOULDER

2-6

READ OVER MY SHOULDER?
JIM DAVIS
© 1979 United Feature Syndicate, Inc.

© 1979 United Feature Syndicate, Inc.

© 1979 United Feature Syndicate, Inc.

© 1979 United Feature Syndicate, Inc.

© 1979 United Feature Syndicate, Inc.

BARK! YIP!
ROWR! FFFT!
JIM DAVIS

GARFIELD! ODIE!
WHY DON'T YOU BOYS GO OUTSIDE TO FIGHT
2-14
© 1979 United Feature Syndicate, Inc.

WHILE I LIE HERE AND QUIETLY BLEED TO DEATH

© 1979 United Feature Syndicate, Inc.

GARFIELD! GET OFF THE PIANO!
2-15

TALK ABOUT STIFLING ONE'S CREATIVE TALENTS
JIM DAVIS

THERE'S ONE NICE THING ABOUT BEING A CAT AT THE DINNER TABLE
2-16
© 1979 United Feature Syndicate, Inc.

EVERYTHING YOU TOUCH IS YOURS
JIM DAVIS

WHAT'S A SIX-LETTER WORD FOR "PAIN," GARFIELD?
JIM DAVIS
2-17

ARRRGH!!!
KROCK!

IS THAT WITH THREE OR FOUR R'S?
© 1979 United Feature Syndicate, Inc.

© 1979 United Feature Syndicate, Inc.

YOU SAY YOU WANT ME TO EAT THIS HAMBURGER, POOKY?
© 1979 United Feature Syndicate, Inc.

AND THIS CHICKEN? AND THIS LASAGNA?

YOU GOTTA GO A LONG WAY TO FIND A TEDDY BEAR AS GOOD AS OLD POOKY HERE
2-19
JIM DAVIS

SMACK!
JIM DAVIS

HEY YOU! COME BACK HERE AND FIGHT LIKE A TEDDY BEAR!

WHAT AM I SAYING?
2-20
© 1979 United Feature Syndicate, Inc.

BE HONEST, POOKY. DO YOU THINK I'M GETTING A LITTLE PUDGY AROUND THE MIDDLE?
© 1979 United Feature Syndicate, Inc.

2-21

NOT A LOT OF PERSONALITY, BUT HE CERTAINLY KNOWS WHEN TO KEEP HIS MOUTH SHUT
JIM DAVIS

2-22

A DANCING BEAR?
NEXT TIME, I GET TO LEAD
© 1979 United Feature Syndicate, Inc.
JIM DAVIS

© 1979 United Feature Syndicate, Inc.

© 1979 United Feature Syndicate, Inc.

2-24

© 1979 United Feature Syndicate, Inc.

STAND ASIDE, CAT. I KNOW KARATE!

2-26

AND I KNOW FAST AND FURIOUS
© 1979 United Feature Syndicate, Inc.
JIM DAVIS

© 1979 United Feature Syndicate, Inc.

SOME DAYS I'M JUST NOT IN THE MOOD TO BE ADORED
JIM DAVIS
2-27

© 1979 United Feature Syndicate, Inc.

BE CAREFUL AROUND THIS CLOCK, GARFIELD. IT'S AN OLD FAMILY HEIRLOOM

CRASH!
© 1979 United Feature Syndicate, Inc.

ONE SMALL PUSH FOR CAT, ONE GIANT LEAP FOR GOOD TASTE
JIM DAVIS
3-2

WHERE WERE YOU, GARFIELD? I CALLED YOU AN HOUR AGO FOR DINNER
UH-OH
GARFIELD
JIM DAVIS
© 1979 United Feature Syndicate, Inc.

GARFIELD
KLUNK!

YOU'VE GOT TO GET TO CAT FOOD BEFORE IT SETS UP
GARFIELD
3-3

TIE
TIE

TIE
TIE
TIE

YANK
YANK

LEAP!
JIM DAVIS

SPROING!

BOOGA!
BOOGA!
3-4
© 1979 United Feature Syndicate, Inc.

KLONK!

THAT WAS
A LOT OF
TROUBLE
BUT IT WAS
WORTH IT

ZZZZ
YAWN
© 1979 United Feature Syndicate, Inc.
3-5

ZZZZZ
JIM DAVIS

WHAT A HECK OF A WAY TO START THE WEEK

THE DARN TOASTER ISN'T WORKING AGAIN. I GUESS I'LL HAVE TO FIX IT
© 1979 United Feature Syndicate, Inc.
3-6

WHAM!
WHAM!
WHAM!
WHAM!
WHAM!

FIRST, YOU HAVE TO GET ITS ATTENTION
JIM DAVIS

BREAKFAST IS ON, GARFIELD
© 1979 United Feature Syndicate, Inc.
JIM DAVIS

CARRY ME

SOMETIMES I THINK I CATER TO GARFIELD TOO MUCH
GARFIELD
3-7

© 1979 United Feature Syndicate, Inc.
3-8

THAT'S CALLED DISCO DANCING, GARFIELD
THANK HEAVENS

FOR A MINUTE THERE I THOUGHT HE HAD A LIVE CARP IN HIS JOCKEY SHORTS
JIM DAVIS

GARFIELD, THAT STEELY-EYED COWCAT, ROAMS INTO TOWN
© 1979 United Feature Syndicate, Inc.
3-9

HE MOUNTS HIS FAITHFUL STEED, ODIE

ALL I NEED NOW IS A SUNSET
JIM DAVIS

© 1979 United Feature Syndicate, Inc.
3-10

JUST WHEN YOU THINK YOU'VE SEEN YOUR CAT DO IT ALL...
JIM DAVIS

BUZZZZZZZZZZ
SPLOOSH
SPLUTTER SPLUTTER
FLOP!
3-11
PTOOEY! PTOOEY! PTOOEY!
WIPE WIPE
© 1979 United Feature Syndicate, Inc.
CRASH
IF I ACT CASUAL, MAYBE HE WON'T NOTICE
JIM DAVIS

© 1979 United Feature Syndicate, Inc.
3-12

SWISH!

THE MOUTH IS QUICKER THAN THE HAND
JIM DAVIS

© 1979 United Feature Syndicate, Inc.

KNOCK! KNOCK! KNOCK!

NOBODY HOME
3-13
JIM DAVIS

© 1979 United Feature Syndicate, Inc.

I SUPPOSE I SHOULD LEARN TO LIKE ODIE

BUT I JUST CAN'T RESPECT ANYONE WHO TURNS AROUND THREE TIMES TO LIE DOWN
JIM DAVIS
3-14

© 1979 United Feature Syndicate, Inc.
3-15

HMMM

JUST AS I SUSPECTED. THERE'S A TINY SIGN IN THERE SAYING, "SPACE FOR RENT"
JIM DAVIS

BARK!
BARK!
BARK!

THAT'S GOOD ENOUGH
SCREEE
POOMP!

THANKS FOR THE EXERCISE
PUNT!
3-16
JIM DAVIS
© 1979 United Feature Syndicate, Inc.

© 1979 United Feature Syndicate, Inc.

PAT
PAT
PAT
PAT

YOU DIDN'T SEE THAT
3-17
JIM DAVIS

HMMM, JON'S DRAWING BOARD. HMMM, SOME PAPER. HMMM, SOME INK

I THINK THIS WORLD WOULD BE A NICER PLACE IN WHICH TO LIVE:
IF COUNTRIES COULD SETTLE THEIR DIFFERENCES WITHOUT HURTING ANYBODY.
IF EVERYONE SMILED AT EVEN PEOPLE THEY DIDN'T KNOW

IF NOBODY HAD TO STEAL.
IF PEOPLE LAUGHED MORE.
IF EVERYONE FED THEIR CATS ALL THE LASAGNA THEY COULD EAT.
IF WE ALL TOOK MORE PRIDE IN OUR HOMES AND OUR NEIGHBORHOODS
3-18
© 1979 United Feature Syndicate, Inc.

IF WE RESPECTED OUR SENIOR CITIZENS MORE.
IF THERE WERE NO VIOLENCE IN MOVIES AND TELEVISION.
IF EVERYONE COULD READ AND WRITE.
IF FAMILIES TALKED MORE

IF FRIENDS HUGGED MORE.
IF EVERYONE STOPPED AT LEAST ONCE A WEEK TO STROKE A CAT.
AFTER ALL, WE'RE ALL IN THIS TOGETHER

HEY, GARFIELD

WHAT'S THIS?
OH, JUST SOME PAW PRINTS
JIM DAVIS

I'M GOING TO TEACH YOU TO DO SOME TRICKS THIS WEEK, GARFIELD
OVER MY DEAD BODY
GARFIELD
3-19
© 1979 United Feature Syndicate, Inc.

SING FOR ME, GARFIELD
MROWR!
GARFIELD

VERY GOOD!
THERE WAS A BONE IN MY TUNA PÂTÉ
GARFIELD
JIM DAVIS

GARFIELD, GO FETCH MY PIPE, PAPER AND SLIPPERS
YES, SIR. RIGHT AWAY, SIR...
JIM DAVIS
© 1979 United Feature Syndicate, Inc.

WHERE IS HE?

GARFIELD!
OKAY, OKAY. AS SOON AS I'M DONE WITH THE FINANCIAL SECTION
3-20

ROLL OVER, GARFIELD
YOU GOTTA BE KIDDING
© 1979 United Feature Syndicate, Inc.

IF YOU ROLL OVER, I'LL GIVE YOU A DOUBLE HELPING OF LASAGNA

WHIRRRRRR!
JIM DAVIS
3-21

SPEAK, GARFIELD, SPEAK
© 1979 United Feature Syndicate, Inc.
3-22

WHY, OF COURSE, JON. IS THERE ANY PARTICULAR TOPIC ON WHICH YOU'D LIKE TO CONVERSE?

B-B-B-B-B
JIM DAVIS

SIT UP AND BEG FOR THE KITTY MUNCHY, GARFIELD
3-23

TELL YOU WHAT. YOU GIVE ME THE MUNCHY AND I'LL LET YOU KEEP YOUR FACE

I KNEW WE COULD ARRIVE AT A MUTUALLY ACCEPTABLE COMPROMISE
JIM DAVIS
© 1979 United Feature Syndicate, Inc.

DANCE FOR ME, GARFIELD
NOT A CHANCE
JIM DAVIS
© 1979 United Feature Syndicate, Inc.

IF YOU WON'T, I'M SURE ODIE WOULD BE HAPPY TO

YOU HAVE TO KNOW WHAT MOTIVATES A CAT
THIS IS DEMEANING
TAPPITY TAPPITY
3-24

3-25
© 1979 United Feature Syndicate, Inc.
SIGH
HO HUM
GARFIELD
EVER HAD ONE OF THOSE DAYS WHEN YOU FEEL LIKE YOU'VE SLEPT AND EATEN IT ALL?
JIM DAVIS

AH, IT'S EARLY MORNING FOR THE CAPED AVENGER
RING!
© 1979 United Feature Syndicate, Inc.

THE CAPED AVENGER WHO SEARCHES OUT EVIL WHEREVER IT MAY LURK

THE LATE-MORNING EVIL, THAT IS
3-26
JIM DAVIS

THE CAPED AVENGER SEES FOOD!
© 1979 United Feature Syndicate, Inc.
3-27

IN ORDER TO FIGHT EVIL, THE CAPED AVENGER NEEDS FOOD FOR STRENGTH

LOTS AND **LOTS** OF STRENGTH!
JIM DAVIS

© 1979 United Feature Syndicate, Inc.

THE CAPED AVENGER WILL NOW FLY DOWN AND DESTROY THE EVIL MAILMAN
JIM DAVIS
SPLAT!
I THINK THE CAPED AVENGER IS STARTING TO BELIEVE HIS OWN PRESS RELEASES
© 1979 United Feature Syndicate, Inc.
3-30
THE CAPED AVENGER WILL NOW STEP OUTSIDE TO FIGHT EVIL
3-31
THE CAPED AVENGER WILL NOW STEP INSIDE AND ANNOUNCE HIS RETIREMENT
JIM DAVIS
© 1979 United Feature Syndicate, Inc.

I'M SO BORED

HMMMM

JIM DAVIS
PTUI
TWING!
YIP!
SPLOOSH!

BONK!

KICK!

MUCH BETTER
4-1
© 1979 United Feature Syndicate, Inc.

DID YOU KNOW MOST CATS SHED THEIR WINTER COATS IN WARM WEATHER, GARFIELD?
4-2
© 1979 United Feature Syndicate, Inc.

FUMP!

HMMM MUS' BE SPRING
JIM DAVIS

SPRING IS HERE

THE WARM SPRING SUN IS COAXING TREES TO BUD AND FLOWERS TO BLOOM. FLEDGLING SONGBIRDS ARE TESTING THEIR LILTING VOICES. SOFT SPRING ZEPHYRS ARE WAFTING THE SWEET SCENT OF LILACS. SPRING IS HERE

BIG, FAT HAIRY DEAL
© 1979 United Feature Syndicate, Inc.
4-3
JIM DAVIS

THERE'S NOTHING LIKE A LITTLE SPRING WEATHER TO MAKE ONE FEEL LAZY
4-4
JIM DAVIS

I'D BETTER BE CAREFUL

IF I WERE ANY LAZIER, I COULD SLIP INTO A COMA
© 1979 United Feature Syndicate, Inc.

I LIKE SPRING

THE GRASS IS BACK FROM ITS DORMANCY. THE FLOWERS ARE BACK FROM A LONG WINTER'S REST
© 1979 United Feature Syndicate, Inc.
4-5

AND THE BIRDS ARE BACK FROM MIAMI
JIM DAVIS

© 1979 United Feature Syndicate, Inc.

© 1979 United Feature Syndicate, Inc.

CLICK

I'M GOING TO STARE AT THIS TOASTER UNTIL THE TOAST POPS UP

A WATCHED POT NEVER BOILS, GARFIELD
HUH?
POP
© 1979 United Feature Syndicate, Inc.

SEE?
DRAT... DRAT, DRAT, DRAT, DRAT
JIM DAVIS
4-8

© 1979 United Feature Syndicate, Inc.

© 1979 United Feature Syndicate, Inc.

GARFIELD'S SURE BEEN IN A NASTY MOOD LATELY
WE'LL SEE ABOUT THAT. DO YOU KNOW HOW TO TREAT A MAD CAT?

4-11

WITH GREAT, GREAT RESPECT
JIM DAVIS
© 1979 United Feature Syndicate, Inc.

4-12

ROWR!
FFFT!

I THINK I HURT MYSELF
© 1979 United Feature Syndicate, Inc.
JIM DAVIS

I KNOW YOU'VE BEEN IN A NASTY MOOD THIS WEEK, GARFIELD. MANY OF US OCCASIONALLY FEEL ANGRY FOR NO REASON AT ALL... PSYCHOLOGISTS CALL IT A FREE-FLOATING ANXIETY
GARFIELD
© 1979 United Feature Syndicate, Inc.

SPLAT!
FREE-FLOAT THIS!
GARFIELD
4-13

I WONDER IF THIS EVER HAPPENED TO FREUD
GARFIELD
JIM DAVIS

EASY, BOYS
© 1979 United Feature Syndicate, Inc.

WE LOVE YOU, GARFIELD!

DARN. THAT WAS THE BEST DEEP BLUE FUNK I EVER HAD GOING
4-14
JIM DAVIS

SCRATCH SCRATCH SCRATCH
SCRATCH SCRATCH SCRATCH
© 1979 United Feature Syndicate, Inc.
PAT PAT PAT
SCRATCH SCRATCH
PAT PAT
4-15
SCRATCH SCRATCH
PAT PAT
SCRATCH
PAT
BARK!
YIP!
ROWR!
I DON'T THINK I COULD TAKE MUCH MORE LOVING
JIM DAVIS

LET'S GO CHECK THE MAILBOX, GARFIELD
© 1979 United Feature Syndicate, Inc.

4-16
I LOVE GETTING MAIL

JIM DAVIS
IT'S JUST ANOTHER REMINDER YOU'RE ALIVE
THAT'S A PRETTY HEAVY THOUGHT FOR A MONDAY

HOW ABOUT SOME BOILED CABBAGE FOR LUNCH GARFIELD?
4-17

SWIPE!

OR MAYBE SOME COLESLAW
NOW YOU'RE TALKING
JIM DAVIS
© 1979 United Feature Syndicate, Inc.

ARF! ARF! ARF!
4-18

YIP!
SAD
© 1979 United Feature Syndicate, Inc.
JIM DAVIS

'ATTA BOY, GARFIELD!
SQUEAK!
4-19

GO GET 'IM!
SQUEAK!

JIM DAVIS
TAKE FIVE, LITTLE BUDDY. WE'LL MAKE ANOTHER PASS IN A FEW MINUTES
PUFF PUFF
© 1979 United Feature Syndicate, Inc.

HEE
HEE
4-20

HA! HA!
HA! HA!
POOR LYMAN

HE WOULDN'T BE LAUGHING SO HARD IF HE KNEW ODIE JUST DRANK OUT OF THE TOILET
© 1979 United Feature Syndicate, Inc.
JIM DAVIS

HMMM
© 1979 United Feature Syndicate, Inc.
4-21

JIM DAVIS

HMMMM
HERE, ODIE
4-22
© 1979 United Feature Syndicate, Inc.
YIP!
YIP!
YIP!
JIM DAVIS
GARFIELD! GET OUT OF MY SOCK DRAWER!

4-23
© 1979 United Feature Syndicate, Inc.

CRASH!

IT'S AMAZING THE FUN YOU CAN HAVE WITH A HOOP
JIM DAVIS

GEE, I'D ALMOST FORGOTTEN HOW MUCH FUN IT IS TO HANG ON THE OLD SCREEN DOOR
4-24

© 1979 United Feature Syndicate, Inc.
SLAM!

AND I'D COMPLETELY FORGOTTEN ABOUT THE PAIN
JIM DAVIS

HMMM A WHISTLE
© 1979 United Feature Syndicate, Inc.

MUST BE BROKEN
JIM DAVIS
4-25

CLAWS ARE GREAT
© 1979 United Feature Syndicate, Inc.
4-26

THEY ALLOW US CATS TO WALK RIGHT UP TREES

THERE'S ONLY ONE PROBLEM
JIM DAVIS

© 1979 United Feature Syndicate, Inc.
4-27

POP

THEY DON'T CALL ME "LIGHTNING LIPS" FOR NOTHING
JIM DAVIS

I JUST WANT YOU PEOPLE TO KNOW HOW MUCH WE CATS APPRECIATE YOU. WITHOUT YOU, WHO WOULD FEED US? WHO WOULD LOVE US?
4-28

AND MOST IMPORTANT OF ALL...

WHO WOULD CHANGE OUR KITTY LITTER?
JIM DAVIS
© 1979 United Feature Syndicate, Inc.

GROWL

THE CAT CRAVES FRESH MEAT
4-29

WHAT-HO, THE CAT SENSES UNSUSPECTING QUARRY O'ER YON KNOLL
© 1979 United Feature Syndicate, Inc.
JIM DAVIS

COILING LIKE A SPRING, HE PREPARES TO LUNGE

STEELY SINEWS PROPEL HIM TOWARD HIS HELPLESS PREY

ONCE AGAIN A CAT'S PRIMAL INSTINCTS PROVIDE SUSTENANCE

BOY, I'M STARVED. I THINK I'LL HAVE SAUSAGE, HASH BROWNS AND SOME EGGS OVER EASY
4-30
GOOD MORNING, GARFIELD. HERE'S TUNA AND LIVER SURPRISE!
GARFIELD
THE SAUSAGE AND HASH BROWNS ARE DELICIOUS. BUT I DO BELIEVE THE EGGS ARE A BIT OVER-DONE
GARFIELD
JIM DAVIS
© 1979 United Feature Syndicate, Inc.
GASP! CHOKE!
BRACK! COUGH! HACK!
FLOP!
GARFIELD
5-1
CAN THE MELODRAMATICS, GARFIELD, AND FINISH YOUR LIVER
GARFIELD
JIM DAVIS
© 1979 United Feature Syndicate, Inc.

BURP!
GARFIELD
5-2

THAT WAS RUDE AND CRUDE, GARFIELD. CATS ARE MORE SOPHISTICATED THAN TO SUBMIT TO BELCHING AT THE DINNER TABLE
GARFIELD

BRAACK!
GARFIELD
JIM DAVIS
© 1979 United Feature Syndicate, Inc.

TELL ME WHAT YOU THINK OF MY NEW POEM, GARFIELD
5-3

"MY BUDDY"
I HAVE A BUDDY.
MY BUDDY'S A TOAD.
HE'S KIND OF MUDDY,
HE'S FLAT ON THE ROAD.
BUT, HE IS MY BUDDY,
MY BUDDY TO STAY.
'TIL HE'S PEELED UP
AND SAILED AWAY

GARFIELD?
JIM DAVIS
© 1979 United Feature Syndicate, Inc.

© 1979 United Feature Syndicate, Inc.
5-4

UH-OH, HERE COMES JON!

JIM DAVIS

ARE YOU HUNGRY, ODIE?
© 1979 United Feature Syndicate, Inc.

HERE, HAVE SOME CELERY AND TOMATOES AND RADISHES

GARFIELD!
5-5
JIM DAVIS

PURRRR
PURRR
TAPPITY TAPPITY TAPPITY
TAPPITY TAPPITY TAPPITY
© 1979 United Feature Syndicate, Inc.
5-6
SCRATCH! SCRATCH! SCRATCH! SCRATCH!
GOOD MORNING, SUNSHINE. WELCOME TO ANOTHER GLORIOUS, FUN-FILLED DAY WITH YOUR FAVORITE PET!
I'M SO HAPPY TO OWN A CAT, I COULD JUST THROW UP
JIM DAVIS

HEY, LYMAN. WHERE'S MY BREAD KNIFE?
© 1979 United Feature Syndicate, Inc.
5-7

SLASH!

NEVER MIND
JIM DAVIS

THIS IS TOO GOOD TO BE TRUE
© 1979 United Feature Syndicate, Inc.

BOING!

THAT WAS TOO GOOD TO BE TRUE
JIM DAVIS
5-8

© 1979 United Feature Syndicate, Inc.

© 1979 United Feature Syndicate, Inc.

HELLO, JULIE ? HOW ABOUT A MOVIE TONIGHT ? OH, I SEE. OKAY, GOODBYE
© 1979 United Feature Syndicate, Inc.

DARN, SHE SAID SHE WAS JUST WALKING OUT THE DOOR TO VISIT HER BROTHER IN TOKYO
CLICK
5-11

THAT'S WHAT I CALL BAD TIMING
THAT'S CALLED GETTING SHOT OUT OF THE SADDLE, YOU TURKEY
JIM DAVIS

GARFIELD, YOU'RE GETTING TOO FAT
5-12

I AM NOT GETTING TOO FAT

I'M JUST READY FOR THE NEXT SIZE KITTY BED, THAT'S ALL
© 1979 United Feature Syndicate, Inc.
JIM DAVIS

EAT UP, OL' BUDDY
GARFIELD

HMMMM
MUNCHIES
GARFIELD

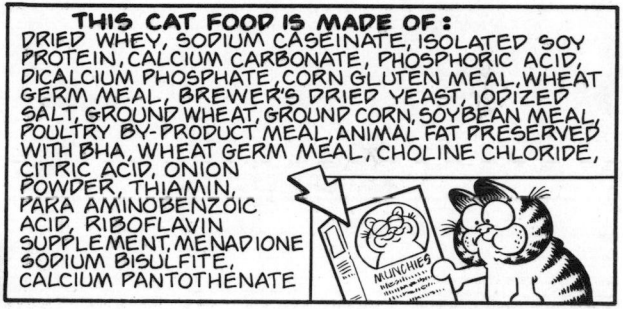
THIS CAT FOOD IS MADE OF:
DRIED WHEY, SODIUM CASEINATE, ISOLATED SOY PROTEIN, CALCIUM CARBONATE, PHOSPHORIC ACID, DICALCIUM PHOSPHATE, CORN GLUTEN MEAL, WHEAT GERM MEAL, BREWER'S DRIED YEAST, IODIZED SALT, GROUND WHEAT, GROUND CORN, SOYBEAN MEAL, POULTRY BY-PRODUCT MEAL, ANIMAL FAT PRESERVED WITH BHA, WHEAT GERM MEAL, CHOLINE CHLORIDE, CITRIC ACID, ONION POWDER, THIAMIN, PARA AMINOBENZOIC ACID, RIBOFLAVIN SUPPLEMENT, MENADIONE SODIUM BISULFITE, CALCIUM PANTOTHENATE
MUNCHIES

NIACIN, IRON SULFATE, MAGNESIUM SULFATE, MANGANESE SULFATE, MANGANOUS OXIDE, ZINC OXIDE, COPPER OXIDE, COBALT CARBONATE
MUNCHIES

YOU WON'T GET RID OF ME THAT EASILY!
GARFIELD

NOW WHAT DID I DO?
GARFIELD
JIM DAVIS
© 1979 United Feature Syndicate, Inc.

5-13

BOY, WHAT A GREAT MEAL

UH-OH!

5-14
GARFIELD
© 1979 United Feature Syndicate, Inc.
JIM DAVIS

IT WAS BOUND TO HAPPEN. MY STOMACH FINALLY OUTGREW MY LEGS
© 1979 United Feature Syndicate, Inc.
5-15

WORSE THINGS COULD HAPPEN, I GUESS

LIKE THIS, FOR INSTANCE
JIM DAVIS

WELL, YOU'VE FINALLY DONE IT, GARFIELD. YOUR BELLY'S BIGGER THAN YOUR LEGS. NOW WHAT ARE YOU GOING TO DO?
© 1979 United Feature Syndicate, Inc.
5-16

I'LL SHOW YOU WHAT I'M GOING TO DO

IF YOU'LL JUST ROLL ME OVER TO THAT LASAGNA THERE
JIM DAVIS

YOU'RE GOING TO HAVE TO EXERCISE THAT BELLY OFF, GARFIELD
© 1979 United Feature Syndicate, Inc.

TELL YOU WHAT. I'LL GET A LEASH AND TAKE YOU FOR A BRISK MORNING DRAG

IF HE HAD A BRAIN, I'D SAY HE WAS TRYING TO MAKE A FUNNY
5-17
JIM DAVIS

© 1979 United Feature Syndicate, Inc.

RIDE 'EM, COWCAT!
BONK!
5-20
© 1979 United Feature Syndicate, Inc.
OH, NO! ODIE'S HURT HIS LEG! WHAT'LL I DO?
SHOOT HIM
JIM DAVIS

I THINK IT'S TIME WE TAKE GARFIELD AND ODIE OUT FOR SOMETHING TO DO
5-21

WHY DO YOU SAY THAT ?

THEY'RE TAKING TURNS ON THE RECORD PLAYER AGAIN
© 1979 United Feature Syndicate, Inc.
JIM DAVIS

CATS CAN BE VERY CURIOUS
ATSUP
5-22

SPLOOCH!
ATSUP

CATS CAN ALSO BE VERY STUPID
© 1979 United Feature Syndicate, Inc.
JIM DAVIS

DID I EVER TELL YOU ABOUT MY UNCLE HARRY? HE WAS A FAMOUS MOUSER AT A GLASS PLANT IN GAS CITY, INDIANA
5-23
© 1979 United Feature Syndicate, Inc.

LEGEND HAS IT THAT UNCLE HARRY CHASED A MOUSE RIGHT INTO TANK #2

NOW HE'S A PAPERWEIGHT IN BAYONNE, NEW JERSEY
JIM DAVIS

GRAB!
JIM DAVIS

BONK!

SMOOTH MOVE, OL' BUDDY
HAVE YOU NO RESPECT FOR THE DEAD?
© 1979 United Feature Syndicate, Inc.
5-24

© 1979 United Feature Syndicate, Inc.

© 1979 United Feature Syndicate, Inc.

DING DONG
—TUG TUG
GOOD EVENING, FELICIA, MY DEAR. DINNER AWAITS
A LOAF OF BREAD, A JUG OF WINE AND THOU (HEH-HEH)
OH, BROTHER
© 1979 United Feature Syndicate, Inc.
WAHCHOO!
I'M ALLERGIC TO CATS! EITHER HE GOES OR I GO
SNIFF!
5-27
POOMP!
GEE, AND SHE WAS CUTE, TOO
SALUD
JIM DAVIS

OH, GOODY. IT'S MONDAY MORNING
BRING!
© 1979 United Feature Syndicate, Inc.

I LOVE MONDAY MORNINGS. YOU KNOW WHY?

BECAUSE I DON'T HAVE TO GO TO WORK
5-28
JIM DAVIS

AH, SIX A.M. TIME TO RISE AND SHINE
BRING!
© 1979 United Feature Syndicate, Inc.

FIRST, A LIGHT BREAKFAST OF JUICE AND TOAST, THEN SOME JOGGING

HA-HA-HA! THAT WAS A GOOD ONE
5-29
JIM DAVIS

Z
© 1979 United Feature Syndicate, Inc.

Z
SMACK
SMACK

OH MY GOSH! I SLEPT THROUGH TODAY'S STRIP!
5-30
JIM DAVIS

THERE'S ONLY ONE DRAWBACK TO SPENDING A WEEK IN BED...
© 1979 United Feature Syndicate, Inc.

SNIFF!

THIS BLANKET IS STARTING TO DEVELOP A PERSONALITY ALL ITS OWN
5-31
JIM DAVIS

GARFIELD, YOU'VE BEEN IN BED ALL WEEK. WHY, YOU COULD STARVE TO DEATH
© 1979 United Feature Syndicate, Inc.

OH

I SHOULD HAVE GUESSED AS MUCH
6-1
JIM DAVIS

GET OUT OF BED THIS MINUTE, GARFIELD
JIM DAVIS
6-2

GOOD BOY!
DARN LEG CRAMPS
© 1979 United Feature Syndicate, Inc.

PTOOEY!

PTOOEY!
6-3
JIM DAVIS

PTOOEY!

OKAY, GARFIELD. NOW GIVE ME SOME HIGH LOBS
© 1979 United Feature Syndicate, Inc.

HAVE A PACKAGE OF CRACKERS, GARFIELD
© 1979 United Feature Syndicate, Inc.

RUSTLE
CRACKLE
CRINKLE

THEY WERE TERRIBLE!
NEXT TIME TRY TAKING THEM OUT OF THE WRAPPER
6-4
JIM DAVIS

WHY THE DROOPY DEMEANOR TODAY, GARFIELD?
© 1979 United Feature Syndicate, Inc.
6-5

KONK!

NEVER SAY "DROOP" TO A FAT PERSON
JIM DAVIS

HEY, LYMAN. WHAT DO YOU THINK OF MY NEW TENNIS RACKET ?

WHAT'S IT STRUNG WITH ?
CATGUT

6-6

© 1979 United Feature Syndicate, Inc.
AUNT REBA!
JIM DAVIS

THAT'S THE TROUBLE WITH WARM WEATHER
JIM DAVIS

YOU CAN'T KEEP ICE CUBES IN YOUR DRINK

© 1979 United Feature Syndicate, Inc.

6-7

TOUCH MY PIE AND YOU DIE
© 1979 United Feature Syndicate, Inc.

TOUCH

ALWAYS RIDING THE RAGGED EDGE OF DISASTER, AREN'T YOU, GARFIELD?!
ZOOM!!!
JIM DAVIS
6-8

WAITRESS, THIS POTATO IS BAD
© 1979 United Feature Syndicate, Inc.

BAD POTATO! BAD POTATO!
SMACK! SMACK! SMACK!

6-9
SIR, IF THAT POTATO GIVES YOU ANY MORE TROUBLE, YOU JUST LET ME KNOW
THERE GOES HER TIP
JIM DAVIS

IT'S ONLY NOON, GARFIELD. WHY DON'T YOU SLEEP IN TODAY. YOU DESERVE THE REST
HEY, GARFIELD! LET'S HAVE SOME FUN! I'LL HOLD ODIE DOWN AND YOU BEAT HIM UP
HOW ABOUT SOME EXERCISE, GARFIELD? WHY DON'T YOU SCRATCH UP MY FAVORITE CHAIR HERE?
6-10
© 1979 United Feature Syndicate, Inc.
DON'T WORRY ABOUT KNOCKING THE PLANTS OFF THE SHELF TODAY, GARFIELD. WE'LL DO IT FOR YOU
CRASH!
CRASH!
I BAKED TONS OF LASAGNA FOR YOU OL' BUDDY. EAT! EAT!
POOF!
WHAT A DEPRESSING DREAM. FOR A MOMENT THERE I THOUGHT ALL THE FUN HAD GONE OUT OF MY LIFE
JIM DAVIS

COME ON, GARFIELD. LET'S GO CAMPING
NOT ON YOUR LIFE
© 1979 United Feature Syndicate, Inc.
JIM DAVIS

GEE, AND I'D PACKED LOTS OF LASAGNA, TOO

SINCE YOU PUT IT THAT WAY, I RECKON THERE'S A TRAIL OR TWO OUT THERE THAT COULD STAND A LITTLE BLAZING
6-11

WELL, HERE WE ARE IN THE GREAT OUTDOORS, GARFIELD

AH, WILDERNESS

JUST US, THE SKY, AND THE TREES
WHERE'S THE TV?
© 1979 United Feature Syndicate, Inc.
6-12
JIM DAVIS

WELL, GARFIELD
© 1979 United Feature Syndicate, Inc.

WHAT DO YOU THINK OF CAMPING SO FAR ?
I DON'T KNOW

I'VE NEVER BEEN THIS FAR FROM THE SANDBOX BEFORE
6-13
JIM DAVIS

WHY THE LONG FACE, GARFIELD?
6-14

LOOK WHO I BROUGHT
POOKY!

CAMPING IS MORE FUN WITH A GOOD FRIEND
© 1979 United Feature Syndicate, Inc.
JIM DAVIS

© 1979 United Feature Syndicate, Inc.

WHAT'S THAT ?

MUST BE A PORCUPINE
6-15
JIM DAVIS

GARFIELD! YOU'RE COVERED WITH PORCUPINE QUILLS!
6-16
© 1979 United Feature Syndicate, Inc.

THAT MUST BE VERY PAINFUL
I CAN HANDLE IT

ARRRRRGH!
JIM DAVIS

SCREW
SCREW
SCREW
LOOK, GARFIELD! I MADE A KITTY DOOR FOR YOU
© 1979 United Feature Syndicate, Inc.
SWING
SMACK!
SMASH!
A CLEAR-CUT CASE OF SELF-DEFENSE IF I EVER SAW ONE
JIM DAVIS
6-17

© 1979 United Feature Syndicate, Inc.

© 1979 United Feature Syndicate, Inc.

HAVE A SAUSAGE
6-20

ONE AT A TIME, GARFIELD, ONE AT A TIME
© 1979 United Feature Syndicate, Inc.
JIM DAVIS

HERE'S TO GLUTTONY!
GARFIELD
© 1979 United Feature Syndicate, Inc.

GULP!
GARFIELD

HELLO? OVEREATERS ANONYMOUS?
JIM DAVIS
6-21

© 1979 United Feature Syndicate, Inc.

© 1979 United Feature Syndicate, Inc.

HOW ABOUT A SNACK, GARFIELD?

HERE'S SOME LIVER LEFT FROM DINNER
BLECH!
6-24

IT'S GOOD. REALLY. WATCH ME

M-M-M-M NUMMY, NUMMY, NUMMY
OH, VERY WELL
© 1979 United Feature Syndicate, Inc.

A MOUSE! GET IT!

GARFIELD, WHY CAN'T YOU CHASE MICE LIKE OTHER CATS?

IF JON EATS ONE FIRST, I'LL CONSIDER IT
JIM DAVIS

I'M GOING TO TAKE YOU TO THE VET FOR A CHECKUP, GARFIELD
OH-NO!
6-25

MY UNCLE BARNEY WENT TO THE VET ONCE

HE CAME BACK AS MY AUNT BERNICE
© 1979 United Feature Syndicate, Inc.
JIM DAVIS

THE DOCTOR WILL SEE YOUR CAT IN A MOMENT
DR. ILSI
6-26

WHO'S NEXT, PLEASE ?

I THINK I JUST DIED AND WENT TO HEAVEN
I THINK I JUST DIED
© 1979 United Feature Syndicate, Inc.
JIM DAVIS

BY THE WAY THERE, DOC, WHAT'S YOUR NAME?
LIZ
© 1979 United Feature Syndicate, Inc.

GEE, WHAT A PRETTY NAME. IS THAT SHORT FOR ELIZABETH?
NO. IT'S SHORT FOR LIZARD

LIZ MUST NOT BE MUCH FOR SMALL TALK
6-27
JIM DAVIS

I GUESS WE'LL BE SEEING A LOT OF EACH OTHER, DOC. GARFIELD GETS SICK A LOT. DON'T YOU, GARFIELD?
JIM DAVIS

DON'T YOU, GARFIELD?

© 1979 United Feature Syndicate, Inc.
KACHEW KACHEW
6-28

WELL, MR. ARBUCKLE, YOUR CAT'S BASICALLY IN GOOD HEALTH

BUT YOU'LL HAVE TO TAKE BETTER CARE OF HIM
LISTEN TO THE DOCTOR, JON
6-29

HE'S TOO FAT
CLOSE YOUR EARS, BOY! THE WOMAN'S SOME KIND OF A QUACK!
JIM DAVIS
© 1979 United Feature Syndicate, Inc.

TELL ME, LIZ, HAVEN'T WE MET SOMEWHERE BEFORE? A RICE PADDY IN HONG KONG?
6-30

LOOK, JERK. I'LL BE THE VET FOR YOUR CAT, BUT I WON'T PLAY FALL GUY FOR YOUR STUPID LINES. UNDERSTOOD?
UH-HUH

SO LONG, DOCTOR
HAVE A NICE DAY
© 1979 United Feature Syndicate, Inc.
JIM DAVIS

BARK!
POW!
POW!
CRACK!
CRASH!
GRRRR
THEY DON'T TELL YOU ABOUT THESE THINGS IN THE PET MAGAZINES
© 1979 United Feature Syndicate, Inc.
JIM DAVIS
7-1

YOU'RE TOO FAT, GARFIELD
7-2

WHY, I'LL BET YOU HAVEN'T SEEN YOUR FEET IN YEARS

I HAVE FEET?
JIM DAVIS
© 1979 United Feature Syndicate, Inc.

CRUNCH
JIM DAVIS

I THINK IT'S TIME I PUT YOU ON ANOTHER DIET, GARFIELD

WHATEVER GAVE HIM THAT IDEA?
7-3
© 1979 United Feature Syndicate, Inc.

I'M STARTING YOUR DIET, GARFIELD
7-4
© 1979 United Feature Syndicate, Inc.

HOW WOULD YOU LIKE THIS HEAD OF CABBAGE PREPARED?
DEEP-FRY THAT SUCKER

BOILED IT IS
WHAT WE HAVE HERE IS A FAILURE TO COMMUNICATE
JIM DAVIS

HMMM, DIET CANDY
CANDY
7-5
© 1979 United Feature Syndicate, Inc.

NOT BAD

A COUPLE MORE BOXES OF THOSE THINGS AND I'LL BE SKINNIER THAN A RAIL
JIM DAVIS

THIS DIET I'M ON HAS SURE MADE ME WEAK
© 1979 United Feature Syndicate, Inc.
7-6

PUNT!

DRAT, HE USUALLY CLEARS THE PIANO
JIM DAVIS

I WONDER WHAT I'D LOOK LIKE SKINNY?
© 1979 United Feature Syndicate, Inc.

GARFIELD! YOUR DIET!
MY VANITY
JIM DAVIS 7-7

© 1979 United Feature Syndicate, Inc.

CATS ARE THE WORLD'S GREATEST TREE CLIMBERS
© 1979 United Feature Syndicate, Inc.

THERE'S ONLY ONE TINY PROBLEM...

CATS ARE ALSO THE WORLD'S WORST TREE CLIMBER DOWNERS
7/9
JIM DAVIS

I'VE MADE UP MY MIND. THE ONLY WAY OUT OF THIS TREE IS TO JUMP. I MAY BREAK EVERY BONE IN MY BODY, BUT HERE GOES
© 1979 United Feature Syndicate, Inc.

THEN AGAIN...
7-10
JIM DAVIS

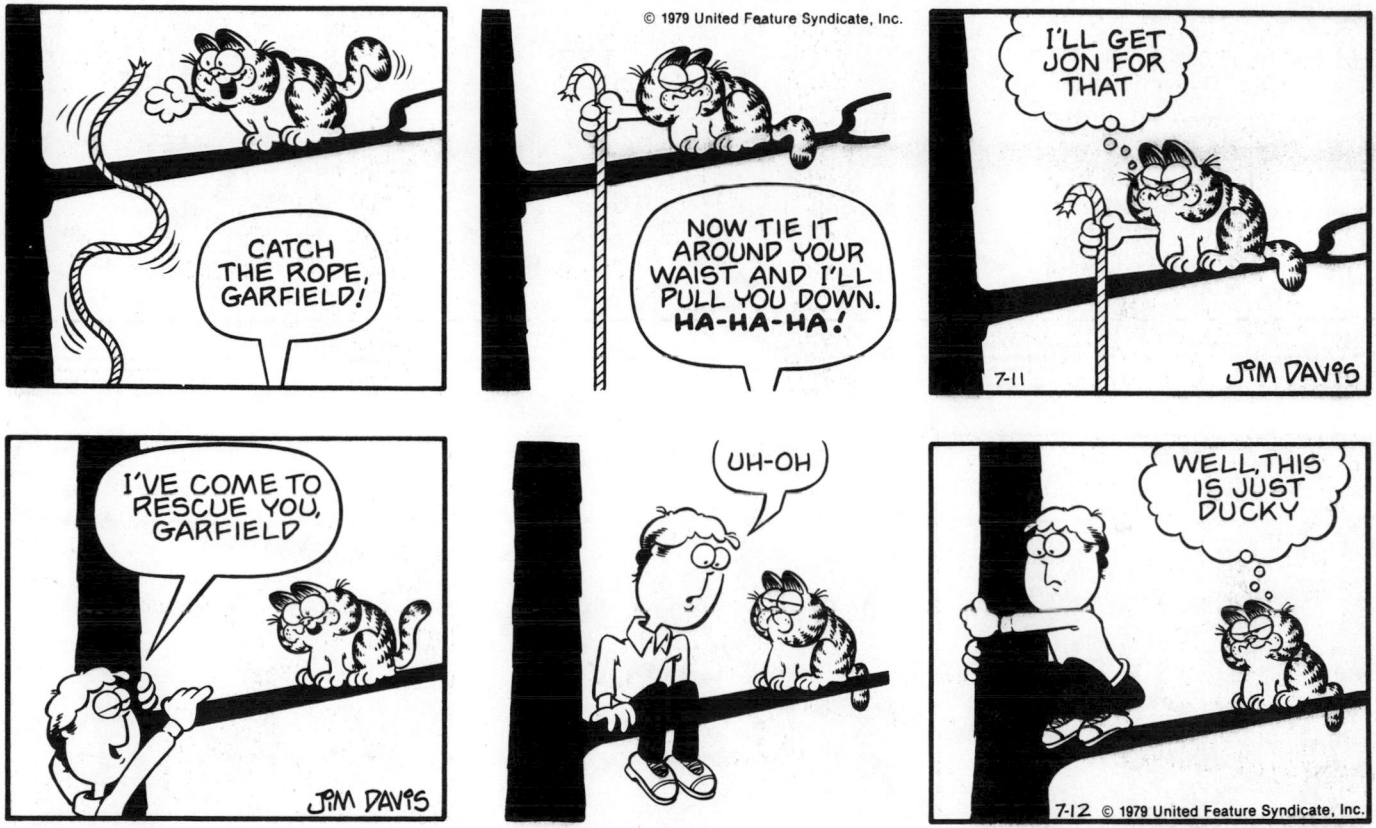
CATCH THE ROPE, GARFIELD!
© 1979 United Feature Syndicate, Inc.
NOW TIE IT AROUND YOUR WAIST AND I'LL PULL YOU DOWN. HA-HA-HA!
I'LL GET JON FOR THAT
7-11
JIM DAVIS
I'VE COME TO RESCUE YOU, GARFIELD
JIM DAVIS
UH-OH
WELL, THIS IS JUST DUCKY
7-12 © 1979 United Feature Syndicate, Inc.

THERE'S ONLY ONE WAY OUT OF THIS TREE, GARFIELD
7-13
JIM DAVIS

WE'LL HAVE TO JUMP

GEE, I'D LOVE TO BUT I SIMPLY HAVEN'T A THING TO WEAR TO OUR FUNERAL
© 1979 United Feature Syndicate, Inc.

EITHER WE JUMP, OR WE'LL STARVE UP HERE, GARFIELD
I'M WITH YOU
JIM DAVIS

GERONIMO!!

© 1979 United Feature Syndicate, Inc.
7-14

AHEM... ME, ME, MEEE
♪MEYOWRRR♫
7-15
BONK
I WONDER IF THIS IS HOW ENRICO CARUSO GOT HIS START
© 1979 United Feature Syndicate, Inc.
♪MEYOWRRRR♫
CLOBBER!!
CLINK CLINK CLANK
♪MEYOWRR♫
BINK
JIM DAVIS

ZOOM!
© 1979 United Feature Syndicate, Inc.
7-16

WHY, OH WHY, OH WHY, OH WHY, DO CATS DO THESE THINGS?
JIM DAVIS

I'M GETTING OUT OF THIS TREE IF IT KILLS ME
7-17

POOMP!

GEE, THAT DIDN'T HURT AT ALL
© 1979 United Feature Syndicate, Inc.
JIM DAVIS

WHAT ARE YOU DOING WITH THE ICE PICK, GARFIELD?
© 1979 United Feature Syndicate, Inc.
7-18

STAB STAB STAB STAB STAB

THE ONLY WAY TO EAT PEAS
OH
JIM DAVIS

WELL, HELLO THERE, GOOD-LOOKING
© 1979 United Feature Syndicate, Inc.
7-19

SAY, WHAT'RE YOU DOING TONIGHT?

HOW ABOUT COMING TO MY PLACE FOR DINNER?
JIM DAVIS

SAY, HOW ABOUT POPPING OVER TO MY PLACE FOR A LATE-NIGHT SNACK?
© 1979 United Feature Syndicate, Inc.
7-20

HA-HA-HA. YOU NEEDN'T BE AFRAID OF LITTLE OL' ME

IF YOU LIKE, YOU CAN BRING A FRIEND AND WE'LL HAVE DESSERT, TOO
JIM DAVIS

I'M SORRY. WE DON'T SERVE CATS HERE
© 1979 United Feature Syndicate, Inc.

WHAT WILL YOU AND YOUR DOG HAVE, SIR ?
7-21
JIM DAVIS

GO GET 'IM, GARFIELD!
OOPS!
SQUEAK!
EVERYONE STAND BACK! GIVE HIM SOME AIR!
ARTIFICIAL RESPIRATION MIGHT HELP
7-22
© 1979 United Feature Syndicate, Inc.
OKAY, GO, BOY
PHEW! FOR A MINUTE THERE I THOUGHT I WAS OUT OF A JOB
JIM DAVIS

© 1979 United Feature Syndicate, Inc.

HOW ABOUT A DATE, SWEETHEART?
© 1979 United Feature Syndicate, Inc.
JIM DAVIS

THAT'S DOCTOR TO YOU
7-25

OKAY, HOW ABOUT A DATE, DOCTOR SWEETHEART?

TELL ME, DOC
© 1979 United Feature Syndicate, Inc.

DO YOU MAKE HOUSE CALLS?
7-26

IT'S NOT THE VETERINARY MEDICINE I MIND. IT'S SOME OF THE ANIMALS I HAVE TO WORK WITH
JIM DAVIS

© 1979 United Feature Syndicate, Inc.

CRASH!
7-29
SMASH!
© 1979 United Feature Syndicate, Inc.
LEAP!
SPLAT!
TAKE THAT!
JIM DAVIS

7-30

ZOOM!

HOW DO THEY KNOW WHEN IT'S BATH DAY?
JIM DAVIS
© 1979 United Feature Syndicate, Inc.

BATH TIME!
© 1979 United Feature Syndicate, Inc.
7-31

CHUCKLE CHUCKLE
SOAP

OKAY, WHO PUT OATMEAL IN THE SOAPBOX?
WELL, SPRINKLE ME WITH BROWN SUGAR AND CALL ME FOR BREAKFAST
JIM DAVIS

WHY CAN'T YOU BE LIKE OTHER CATS, GARFIELD?
JIM DAVIS
8-1

LET ME EXPLAIN THE BASIC DIFFERENCES BETWEEN HUMANS AND CATS

WELL, MAKE IT SNAPPY. I HAVE A TENNIS LESSON IN HALF AN HOUR
© 1979 United Feature Syndicate, Inc.

TIME FOR A MIDNIGHT SNACK
CEREAL
8-2
© 1979 United Feature Syndicate, Inc.

CRINKLE
CEREAL

CEREAL
JIM DAVIS

BOING
BOING
BOING
8-3
NG
BOING
BOING
HELP!
BOING
BOING
© 1979 United Feature Syndicate, Inc.
JIM DAVIS
FOR STAYING OUT OF MY FOOD TODAY, GARFIELD, I'M GOING TO REWARD YOU WITH A KITTY MUNCHIE
KITTY MUNCHIE
© 1979 United Feature Syndicate, Inc.
KITTY MUNCHIE
8-4
THEY'RE GONE
I ALREADY REWARDED MYSELF
KITTY MUNCHIE
JIM DAVIS

8-5
© 1979 United Feature Syndicate, Inc.
WHAT SAY I SWITCH OVER TO THE MOVIE, GANG?
NAH
GRRR
FFFT
JIM DAVIS

© 1979 United Feature Syndicate, Inc.

GARFIELD'S HISTORY OF CATS:
DURING THE DARK AGES THE LEGENDARY RATTER "FLUFFY-THE-FIERCE" DESTROYED EVERY RAT BUT ONE...
SQUEAK!
JIM DAVIS

OL' FLUFFY GOT HIS CLOCK CLEANED BY THE EVEN MORE LEGENDARY "MATT-THE-RAT"
DRIBBLE
DRIBBLE
DRIBBLE

INCIDENTALLY, IT WAS MATT-THE-RAT WHO COINED THE TERM "HERE, KITTY, KITTY, KITTY"
© 1979 United Feature Syndicate, Inc.
8-8

GARFIELD'S HISTORY OF CATS:
MARCO POLO HAD A CAT NAMED ROLO
ROLO POLO
8-9
© 1979 United Feature Syndicate, Inc.

ROLO WOULD HAVE GONE WITH MARCO ON HIS TRIP TO THE ORIENT...

BUT MOTELS WOULDN'T ACCEPT PETS THEN
WAH!
JIM DAVIS

GARFIELD'S HISTORY OF CATS:
A CAT DISCOVERED AMERICA!

IT WAS CHRISTOPHER COLUMBUS' CAT "BUCKEYE" WHO FIRST SPOTTED THE BEACH

PRIMARILY BECAUSE THE SANTA MARIA DIDN'T HAVE A SANDBOX
© 1979 United Feature Syndicate, Inc.
8-10
JIM DAVIS

GARFIELD'S HISTORY OF CATS:
CATS' PENCHANT FOR SHARPENING THEIR CLAWS HAS SERVED MANY HISTORIC PURPOSES:
IN VICTORIAN TIMES CATS WERE USED TO ANTIQUE FURNITURE
RRRRRRR
8-11

DURING THE SPANISH-AMERICAN WAR, CATS WERE USED AS INTERROGATORS
I'LL TALK!
I'LL TALK!
© 1979 United Feature Syndicate, Inc.

AND TODAY, THE POST OFFICE USES CATS TO SORT MAIL MARKED "FRAGILE"
JIM DAVIS

BOY, IT'S HOT!
CHIRP CHIRP WHEEE!
OUT, BIRDS. OUT, OUT, OUT
© 1979 United Feature Syndicate, Inc.
8-12
SHARKS!
JIM DAVIS

OH, GARFIELD! COME AND...
GARFIELD
8-13
© 1979 United Feature Syndicate, Inc.

ZOOM!

GET IT
GARFIELD
JIM DAVIS

HMMM A DOGGIE BISCUIT
DOGGIE BISCUIT
8-14

WHAT A DISAPPOINTMENT

THAT DOESN'T TASTE AT ALL LIKE DOGGIE
JIM DAVIS
© 1979 United Feature Syndicate, Inc.

ONE THING I ADMIRE IN CATS IS THEIR NATURAL GRACE
© 1979 United Feature Syndicate, Inc.
8-15

SMACK!

AND THEN THERE'S GARFIELD
JIM DAVIS

HMM
8-16

JIM DAVIS
© 1979 United Feature Syndicate, Inc.

YESTERDAY I STUFFED ODIE'S NOSE IN HIS MOUTH
© 1979 United Feature Syndicate, Inc.

YOU SHOULD HAVE SEEN HIM...

RUNNING AROUND IN LITTLE CIRCLES GOING "MARK! MARK! MARK!"
JIM DAVIS
8-17

OH BOY, WHAT A NIGHT. I ATE TOO MUCH, I DRANK TOO MUCH, AND I DANCED HALF THE NIGHT
© 1979 United Feature Syndicate, Inc.

YOU'RE LUCKY YOU'RE A CAT, GARFIELD. YOU DON'T HAVE TO PUT UP WITH ALL THAT

RUB IT IN, WHY DON'T YOU?!
JIM DAVIS
8-18

YAWN!
YAWN

LA LA LA ♪
MROW ♪
JIM DAVIS

GARFIELD

STROKE
STROKE
STROKE

COME ON, GARFIELD. LET'S GO JOGGING
HAVE A GOOD TIME
© 1979 United Feature Syndicate, Inc.
8-19

HAVE YOU EVER THOUGHT ABOUT MEETING SOME NICE GIRL CAT AND SETTLING DOWN, GARFIELD?
NOT REALLY
8-20

WE BOY CATS CHERISH OUR BACHELORHOOD

WHY, I COME FROM A LONG LINE OF BACHELORS
JIM DAVIS
© 1979 United Feature Syndicate, Inc.

© 1979 United Feature Syndicate, Inc.
8-21

JIM DAVIS

© 1979 United Feature Syndicate, Inc.

© 1979 United Feature Syndicate, Inc.
8-24

YOU WIN. YOU WERE UGLIER TO BEGIN WITH
JIM DAVIS

8-25
I'M NEVER TAKING YOU GOLFING AGAIN, GARFIELD
BIG DEAL
© 1979 United Feature Syndicate, Inc.

I'VE NEVER BEEN SO EMBARRASSED

I CAN'T BELIEVE WHAT YOU DID AT THE SEVENTEENTH GREEN
SAND TRAP, SANDBOX, WHAT'S THE DIFFERENCE?
JIM DAVIS

WE'RE GOING FOR A WALK, GARFIELD
I HATE LEASHES
HEH, HEH. TAKING YOUR PET FOR A STROLL THROUGH THE PARK IS A GREAT WAY TO MEET CHICKS
GRRR FFFT
8-26
© 1979 United Feature Syndicate, Inc.
ROWRR!
WHAT KIND OF A JERK WOULD WALK HIS CAT ON A LEASH?
ROWR!
ROWR! FFFT!
YIP! YIP! YIP!
JIM DAVIS
BACK TO THE DRAWING BOARD

A Talk with Jim Davis:
Most Asked Questions

How far in advance do you do the strip?

"Eight to ten weeks—no less, no more. I operate on what Al Capp termed 'the ragged edge of disaster.'"

When did GARFIELD first appear in newspapers?

"June 19, 1978."

Do you own a cat? A GARFIELD?

"No. My wife, Carolyn, is allergic to cats. However, I did grow up on a farm with about 25 cats."

Where do you get your ideas for the strip?

"I glean a lot of good ideas from fan mail. Cat owners are very proud of their cats and supply a generous amount of cat stories."

What GARFIELD products are on the market and in production?

"Books, calendars, T-shirts, coffee mugs, posters, tote bags, greeting cards, puzzles...in another few months GARFIELD will be on everything but pantyhose and TVs."

Why a cat?

"Aside from the obvious reasons, that I know and love cats, I noticed there were a lot of comic-strip dogs who were commanding their share of the comic pages but precious few cats. It seemed like a good idea."

Where did you get the name GARFIELD?

"My grandfather's name was James A. Garfield Davis. The name GARFIELD to me sounds like a fat cat...or a St. Bernard...or a neat line of thermal underwear."

What did you do for a living before GARFIELD?

"I was assistant on the comic strip TUMBLEWEEDS and a free-lance commercial artist."

What's your sign?

"Leo, of course, the sign of the cat."

Have you ever been convicted of a felony?

"Next question, please."

Are you subject to fainting spells, seizures, and palpitations?

"Only when I work."

Have you ever spent time in a mental institution?

"Yes, I visit my comics editor there."

Do you advocate the overthrow of our government by violent means?

"No, but I have given consideration to vandalizing my local license branch."

Are you hard of hearing?

"Huh?"

Do you wish to donate an organ?

"Heck no, but I have a piano I can let go cheap."